From the Farm to the Table
Beef

by

Kathy Coatney

Copyright @ 2015 by Kathy Coatney

www.kathycoatney.com

From the Farm to the Table Series
From the Farm to the Table: Beef
Book 6

All rights reserved

No part of this publication can be reproduced or transmitted in any form or by any means, electonic or mechanical, without permission in writing from Kathy Coatney

CONTENTS

Dedication . . . . Pg iv

Acknowledgements . . . . Pg 1

From the Farm to the Table Beef. . . . . Pg 3

Vocabulary . . . . Pg 27

Author Biography . . . . Pg 28

Dedication

Thanks to Rancher Mary for her time and expertise.

Acknowledgements

I've had a number of life-altering moments in my life, each special in their own way. The road to becoming a children's author has been smooth and rocky, but it has been an incredible journey because of those who have accompanied me.

My inspiration for the project, Georgia Bockoven; email check-in pals, Jennifer Skullestad and Lisa Sorensen; and critique partner Luann Erickson, you are my GPS to finding the end. Friends and family who made the journey memorable: Karol Black, Tammy Lambeth, Libby Hall, Shari Boullion, Diana Robertson, Terry McLaughlin, and Patti Berg, and my family — Nick, Wade and Devin, Jake and Emily and sweet little Allie. I'm blessed to have had you all beside me.

I've also had the pleasure to work with several talented businesswomen: Susan Crosby, my editor; Yvonne Betancourt, my formatter, and Tara, my cover designer.

Note to parents and teachers: The underlined words are second-grade vocabulary words.

From the Farm to the Table Series

From the Farm to the Table: Dairy
From the Farm to the Table: Bees
From the Farm to the Table: Olives
From the Farm to the Table: Potatoes
From the Farm to the Table: Almonds
From the Farm to the Table: Beef

From the Farm to the Table: Beef

Rancher Mary is a cow gal. When she was a little girl she lived on a dairy with her parents and brothers and sisters.

After Rancher Mary grew up, she began raising beef cattle. She moved to her <u>ranch</u> that is <u>nestled</u> at the base of Mt. Shasta in northern California.

Photo Courtesy of Mary Rickert

Farmers that raise beef cattle are called <u>ranchers</u>. Beef cattle are very important, and they are used to make all kinds of things, from food to piano keys.

Photo Courtesy of Mary Rickert

<u>Beef</u> has lots of protein that is good food for us to eat and makes strong bones and muscles.

Beef makes some of Rancher Mary's favorite foods-homemade hamburgers and hotdogs straight from the BBQ, and her favorite, beef stew with loads of vegetables.

Photo Courtesy of Mary Rickert

The <u>entire</u> cow is used, and nothing goes to waste. Fats from cattle are made into oleo oil for margarine and shortening. Oleo stearin is used to make chewing gum.

Photo Courtesy of Mary Rickert

Gelatin produced from bones and skins is used in marshmallows and ice cream. The leather from cow hide is made into shoes, coats, baseballs and footballs.

Photo Courtesy of Mary Rickert

The bones, horns and hooves are used to make things like buttons, bone china, piano keys, glues, and fertilizer.

<u>Herds</u> are groups of cattle, and Rancher Mary has a very special herd called a <u>closed herd.</u>

A closed herd means no other cows are brought in from another herd. They are all born and raised in the herd.

Rancher Mary has the largest closed herd in the United States, and it took 25 years to build the herd.

Rancher Mary's closed herd are used to make very special things. Instead of steel plates and screws commonly used in joint replacement surgeries, cow bones are used.

Collagen comes from the cow hide. It is made into <u>amazing</u> things like spray-on bandages and surgical sutures. Sutures are used to close an incision after an operation.

Photo Courtesy of Mary Rickert

Collagen has other surprising uses. Collagen dressings are used on second-degree burns and skin grafts.

Rancher Mary getting ready to vaccinate cows

The cattle are <u>examined</u> regularly by the veterinarian, a doctor for animals, to make sure they aren't sick and to give them vaccinations to keep them strong and healthy.

All the cattle in Rancher Mary's herd graze on <u>certified organic pastures</u>. Her pastures were <u>inspected</u> to guarantee they hadn't been chemically treated for disease and pests.

Rancher Mary's ranch is also certified by <u>Humane Farm Animal Care</u>.

Certification requires that Rancher Mary's cattle are treated well, receive an abundance of fresh water, and have plenty of space to roam and graze.

Rancher Mary is very proud that her cattle are used to make so many important things.

Photo Courtesy of Mary Rickert

Cattle eat alfalfa hay, so Rancher Mary also grows alfalfa. Deer and antelope love to graze on the alfalfa, too, so she grows enough for the cattle, and the deer and antelope.

Rancher Mary checking the water trough

Raising beef cattle takes a lot of time and hard work. Rancher Mary has lots of chores to do every day.

Tractor cutting hay

Rancher Mary's chores vary from day to day. Some days the cattle are moved to new fields. Other days there is hay to cut.

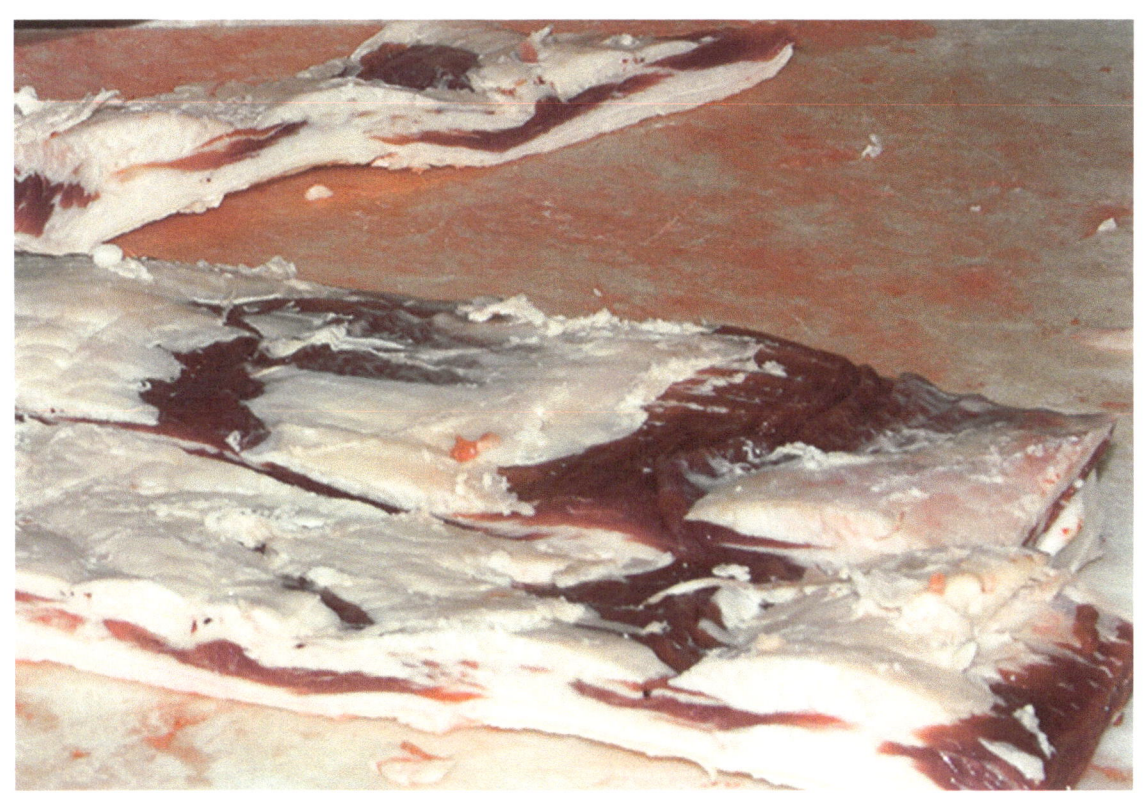

Beef being prepared for sale

Meeting customers at farmers markets is one of Rancher Mary's favorite jobs, but she <u>especially</u> loves knowing she sells good, nutritious food for her customers to eat.

Rancher Mary <u>prefers</u> working outside in the fresh air where she is <u>surrounded</u> by wildflowers and the green <u>meadows</u> where her cattle graze.

Photo Courtesy of Mary Rickert
Rancher Mary with her grandchildren

Raising cattle when it's burning hot in the summer and freezing cold in the winter is the best job in the world, and Rancher Mary wouldn't consider doing anything else!

The End

Vocabulary Word List

Amazing
Chores
Entire
Especially
Examined
Inspected
Meadows
Nestled
Prefers
Surrounded

Author Biography

Kathy Coatney has spent long hours behind the lens of a camera wading through rice paddies, dairies and orchards during her twenty-five year career as a photojournalist specializing in agriculture. She and her husband grow table olives and her family roots in agriculture run four generations deep, so Kathy knows farming from the ground up. Concerned that kids today don't have the exposure to farms and rural life that teaches them how their food is produced, she envisioned a new direction for her writing and launched From the Farm to the Table, a series of nonfiction children's books about agriculture. Kathy also loves — and writes — deeply emotional, small-town contemporary romances.

Visit her website at: www.kathycoatney.com

www.ingramcontent.com/pod-product-compliance
Lightning Source LLC
Chambersburg PA
CBHW050758110526
44588CB00002B/38